I STRONGLY CRAVE
YOUR EXISTENCE

By

Robert Alex

Copyright © Robert Alex, 2022, All Right Reserved

TABLE OF CONTENT

INTRODUCTION

Limerence is a psychological state that can be brought on by romantic or non-romantic feelings for another person. It usually includes obsessive reading and fantasies, as well as the desire to meet the love of one's life and have those passions reciprocated in a relationship.A state of violent, irrational desire is another definition of limerence.

She came up with the idea that it is the experience of being in love while conducting interviews with over 500 people about love in the middle of the 1960s.Limerence, which is not just sexual, has been defined in terms of its connection to the attachment proposition and its implicit capacity to inspire.According to Willmott and Bentley, an involuntary and potentially inspiring state of adoration and attachment to a limerent object (LO) that involves protrusive and compulsive studies, passions, and actions ranging from swoon to despair, depending on perceived emotional negotiation.

According to the attachment proposition, many of the most violent feelings arise during the conformation, conservation, dislocation, and renewal of attachment connections. The conscious experience of sexual instigation or provocation is the state of limerence.

Do you ever have the desire to constantly be touched or the feeling that you can't get enough love?

Keep in mind that doing so is completely normal.In point of fact, people are wired to want to be touched.
Touch starvation, also known as skin hunger or touch deprivation, is more common than you might think. This means that other living things rarely or never touch you.

However, a strong emotional or physical desire for affection can sometimes indicate an excessive reliance on others for one's own well-being, in addition to being touch-starved.Even love addiction, also known as attachment regulation, could be a sign.

If you think you can't live without affection, read on to find out why and how you can learn to control your emotions.The first and most obvious cause of your desire for affection is a lack of affection in your life.You may have been alone for some time without a physical or emotional connection.This affected many people during the most recent pandemic.

If you've ever typed in questions like "does love exist?" into search engines, you're not alone, or "Does love exist?" You might be trying to figure out how you feel about someone. However, since "love" can be experienced and expressed in a variety of ways, it is difficult to define.It could be something written in the stars or just lust and attraction for some of us, while for others, it could be an intense, powerful feeling or chemistry they have with another person.

We all seem to want it, and it's an exciting feeling. But does it really exist, or is it just a social contrast we're told is real?
We can look to science to see what happens to our bodies when we experience this feeling that we all refer to as love in order to determine whether or not

love actually exists.This is what happens in our bodies when we experience that intense feeling, if love exists.
Your brain, not your heart, is where it is.

According to scientific evidence, the feeling of love does not occur in our hearts, contrary to popular belief.Instead, it occurs in our brain when we release hormones that produce a variety of emotions, including oxytocin, dopamine, adrenaline, testosterone, estrogen, and vasopressin:happiness, closeness, or euphoria
The amygdala, at the center of our emotions, is located in the temporal lobe of the limbic system of the brain.This is where hormones are processed and feelings like fear, rage, desire, and love are released. Because it is linked to feelings of attachment and bonding, some people call oxytocin the "love hormone."

Because of the similar levels of dopamine released, some scientists suggest that falling in love is similar to becoming addicted.Your brain releases the hormone when you fall in love, giving you a rush similar to when you take a cocaine high.

You might fall deeply in love (or infatuated) with another person because, like cocaine, your brain becomes addicted to the satisfying feeling of "love" and wants to keep the source of it around. Your body will also experience withdrawal in the event of a breakup or the loss of a loved one.

Does love exist then?

Love is difficult to define because infatuation and love are not the same thing. Some contend that love is a social construct created by the media, while others assert that it is a biological construct that we are all born with.

Since there hasn't been any hard evidence to prove that love is real or just made up and exists in our minds, the scientific study of love is still ongoing. However, one thing we can say is that when these feelings of love are studied, researchers find that parts of our brain and the reward system are working.

In addition to a desire for physical contact, there are a number of other factors that can contribute to a desire for loveandaffection. You can't satisfy your jones indeed if you have loved and watched for people inyourlife.In this case, your desire for affection may point to commodity more fundamental.

CHAPTER ONE

When You Don't Have Affection Growing Up
People who crave a lot of love constantly didn't get enough of itaskids.Sadly, these people may go through life with the strong desire to be held, loved, and appreciated and the conviction that they do notearnlove.Consequently, they may seek tone- love from others in an trouble to heal their injuries and compensate for the lackofaffection.

Love jones can also be brought on by love dependence or attachment dysregulation, which involves obsessive conduct towardotherpeople.Most of the time, it comes from ways of surviving that you learned as a child or from a particularly stressful situation in your life where you had to learn to accept feeling neglected and abandoned.
You might have attachment dysregulation and need to address it if you suppose that other people don't love you enough, worry that they might leave you, or are worried about your relationship.

Who are the characteristics of people who worry for love?

People who have violent love jones constantly parade the following characteristics;

Obsession with love and affection People who want love constantly are unfit to allow it to come to them naturally and come anxious when they do not admit it. Do you believe that affection is too important to you to the point where you sometimes feel like nothing fresh matters?

behavior control People who are showing you love and affection may also act in a controlling and jealous manner when you are in need of love. This may be a means of avoiding suffering and abandonment.

Prayer and soliciting for love Similar to this, you might be more likely to demand affection from others if you place a high value on it.

You could also pray to them to show you the love you so desperately want.

Trust issues A person who has been abandoned or neglected may have a delicate time erecting connectionsthatlast.They might be suspicious and constantly anticipate conspiracies, ulterior motives, and hidden calendars because they are hysterical of being hurt.

Accepting bad behavior.Unfortunately, those who warrant affection may be more likely to tolerate abusive behavior

from those they bond with.Additionally, they might struggle to separate between arguments and abusive situations.

CHAPTER TWO

Understanding why you have developed an obsessive need for attention is a good first step toward developing connections that are further stable. You can try this on your own or talk to an perceptive relationship coach who can help you understand and begin to healyourwounds.As a result of tone- love and acceptance, you will begin to calculate lower on others for affection and further on yourself, laying a healthier foundation for future connections.

- **What can I do to stop wanting love and affection?**

Fortunately, you can ply farther control over your love life and reduce your reliance on other people.Some recommendations   Include the exertion you enjoy most.

Consider thisMake a list of your interests and hobbies. What exertion do you enjoy doing alone? What brings joy?Take note of them and suppose about other options you might like to try.

Suppose about the good goods about yourself.

Write down what you like about yourself, whether it's physical or more character-related.Whatever it is, rather of dwelling on your excrescencies, concentrate on the positive aspects of your personality. Are you secure, compassionate, or kind? Or are you logical, motivated, and responsible?

Enhance wherever possible. suppose about the aspects of your life that you can and cannot change.Accept what you can't control and work to meliorate whatyoucan.Let's say you want to perform better at work but are unfit to change your master's behavior.However, you would put in a lot of trouble to acquire new capacities and establish applicable boundaries in the factory, If that werethecase.You can, if necessary, switch jobs after learning how to plump for yourself and establish applicable factory boundaries.

Give it some time recovering confidence and knowledge to love yourself take time and effort.Instead of putting too important pressure on yourself to change, concentrate on each step atatime.It's possible that if you try to do everything at formerly, you'll feel overwhelmed and indeed give up onyourjourney.Instead, give yourself time to work on yourself, your connections, and your mending one step at a time.

- **Learn how to deal with love addiction at a PIVOT retreat.**

We at PIVOT use our extensive expertise to help people like you heal from childhood wounds and build stronger relationships.If you need help overcoming relationship guilt, are worried that your relationship is falling apart, or feel like you are not being heard, call us.Take advantage of one of our thoughtful relationship retreats or individual coaching sessions to get started on your healing journey.We are here to listen and assist you in achieving self-love, acceptance, and peace.

The need for love from other people frequently stems from a lack of self-love or self-awareness.You must learn to love yourself if you are constantly under the impression that other people do not love you.It is necessary to break the vicious circle of always wanting love as soon as possible.If you learn to live for yourself and recognize your strengths, the love-hungry cycle will end eventually.You will come to the realization that the love of other people is not necessary for happiness.You might be surprised, and others will do the same if you show yourself real love.

CHAPTER THREE

- **Look at what you enjoy doing.**

To break the vicious cycle of wanting to be loved by other people, you need to know what makes you happy.Write down everything you enjoy doing, including reading and writing.If you don't have a favorite hobby, write down one you've always wanted to try, like knitting or hiking.

Make a list of your favorite characteristics.
Instead of focusing on physical characteristics, think about personality traits.If, for instance, you find that helping others brings you joy, write down that you have a big heart.Only your best qualities should be on the list.

Consider the aspects of your life that you would like to enhance.Instead of focusing on things you can't change, try to improve aspects of your life.Some individuals' financial circumstances are not satisfactory.Others believe that they are too distant from their friends and family.Make a list of everything you think can be improved in your life.

Make a commitment to yourself to focus on yourself and not others.People frequently get caught up in trying to please other people because they believe that giving without receiving is acceptable.If you always try to make other people happy and never take care of yourself, you will end up in trouble.Start working on yourself and making yourself happy instead of concentrating on the people around you.

Concentrate on just one thing at a time.Take a look at the list of changes you want to make and pick one to work on first.Start with a small project and work your way up to larger ones.Before quitting smoking, for instance, start walking every day if you want to feel healthier and smoke.Small successes inspire you to tackle more difficult ones.

Always remember to have fun.Examine your list of potential or current interests.Choose a hobby that you like or would like to try.Engage in the pastime while ignoring the stressful aspects of your life.This is your chance to unwind and pursue your passions.

CHAPTER FOUR

• Restore your self-assurance

Regain your confidence.Examine your list of characteristics.When you're feeling down or angry, remember that you have a list of qualities that show your positive qualities.As you gain confidence, add more positive qualities to the list.

Learn about other people.Once you have regained confidence, put yourself out there.Avoid becoming overwhelmed by the fear that you won't be liked or loved by everyone as you converse with others.Allow other people to enjoy both your company and that of others.

Before you can truly love another person, you must first love yourself.But you need to be open with yourself and do some serious soul searching if you want to know if what you feel for your wife is love or just deep care.

Keep in mind that just because you love someone doesn't mean you're in love with them;You must be in love with your wife in order to truly love her.There are a few steps you can take to find out if you love your wife.Determine your definition of love.Make a list of everything that you consider to be important about love and being in a loving relationship.

Know the difference between love, lust, and infatuation.In contrast to lust, which is about sexual desire, infatuation is an initial intense feeling that does eventually fade.

Inquire about other people's definitions of love and what it means to them.

Write about how you feel about your wife.What interests you? Are there any similarities between you?

Consider the entirety of your relationship.Which of you brings out the best in each other? Can you really be yourself when you're together? How do you talk to each other? Do you always fight?

Evaluate whether you are prepared to accept her as she is.Are you even interested in her flaws?

After considering your responses to these questions and conducting some serious soul searching, you ought to have a better idea of whether you love your wife.

The individual or the relationship.Examples of this include things the person left at your house, poetry you wrote, and movies you watched together.Eliminate any songs that moved you in any way.

Feel the pain caused by the person's death.Even if your relationship never developed and you want to get over your crush, you must take the time to get over what could have been.Recognize the impact this person had on your life and how hard it was to keep your feelings in check.

Recognize that you cannot allow this person's emotions to develop.Farouk Radwan, the author of "How to Get Over Anyone in a Few Days," insists that you must:Make it abundantly clear to your subconscious that it is finished."You must acknowledge that the relationship is over and give up any hope that it will work out.

You should redecorate your bedroom if you spend a lot of time there.Give it a fresh look to go with your new emotional start.Paint the walls, move the bed, buy new sheets, or make other minor adjustments to help yourself get over the relationship.
Spend time with those you care about.Sitting around feeling sorry for oneself is simple.Instead, to regain your perspective and happiness, spend time with positive people.If you require assistance, ask others for it.

Don't make friends with someone you love.When you have a romantic relationship with someone, it can be difficult to return to the "friend zone."Facebook and MySpace should not be used for updates because this applies to interactions that take place in person as well as online.

As long as you are not with the other person or going to places you used to go together, you can go to the gym, the movies, the mall, or anywhere else you want.

CHAPTER FIVE

- CREATE A NEW YOU

Create a new you.After imagining a soap opera about your developing feelings for an inappropriate partner, you probably neglected your own personal development.Take a class in an activity you enjoy, exercise, read, volunteer, or engage in other activities that help you develop your self-esteem.

Go to therapy if you need to.You should consider why you started a romantic relationship with a married man and why you would be willing to eat at their table.Talk to a counselor if you frequently find yourself emotionally involved with partners who are not right for you.

Still, if you're not careful, you could be teaching yourself to fail if you constantly think things like "I can't do this" or "I won't ever be successful."Tone-filling predictions can sabotage your success and trick you into taking actions that prevent you from living a happy life and overcoming adversity.Learning how to alter your studies, improve your tone of voice, and engage in tone-satisfying prognostics that lead to success is the first step toward living the life you want.

Tamara Hill, a family therapist, writes in the article "Children with Severe gestational Problems: A companion for Parents" that internalizing negative tone-talk can make you feel unloved, misunderstood, and in fact empty.when you're feeling down and out, your motivation to keep trying changes.To earn your respect, instead, limit your tone to only positive expressions.Avoid the temptation to downgrade your appearance, accomplishments, or performance in order to avoid tone-filling predictions that are negative.You can set an example for others by treating yourself and others with respect.

Fake It If you are having trouble prostrating dubieties about your interpersonal skills or work performance, do not let a tone-filling vaticination lead you to a negative outcome.

According to psychologist Carolyn Kaufman's article "Using tone- Fulfilling prognostics to Your Advantage," which was published in Psychology Today, you should "fake it until you make it."If you train your mind to think positively about your performance or first impression, it will likely change your geste

Consequently, people may also respond to you more positively when you are confident.You may eventually believe the positive studies and avoid allowing negativity to bring you down, even though it may initially appear false or fake if you continue to play the role.

It can be detrimental to your emotional well-being to have a negative friend who is mean, overly competitive, selfish, critical, or complains too much.When a friend's constant negativity starts to affect your mood or self-esteem, it's okay to step back and take care of yourself, even if it means spending less time with them.But you can't just stop seeing her.

CHAPTER SIX

You have to deal with the emotional toll of breaking up with a friend by reminding yourself that you deserve better.

Step 1: Directly address your concern to your friend.According to psychologist Henry Cloud's advice in "How to Gracefully End a Bad Relationship -- With a Friend, Loved One, or Business Associate",if you want to save the friendship, give him a warning and some feedback.

He might not be aware of how emotionally draining his negativity can be.You could say something like, "When I go out with my friends, I just want to have a good time and be in a happy mood.""Your constant complaining affects my stress levels.It would be wonderful if you could try to be more upbeat when we hang out.

Stage 2: Reduce correspondence for an unspecified amount of time.You are free to gradually remove your friend from your life, but you are not required to do so immediately.Irene S. Levine, a psychologist, writes in her book "Ending a friendship nicely" that you shouldn't start new conversations or hangouts with her, but if you do, be friendly and courteous.

Step 3: Keep yourself busy and occupied.In "Anxiety, Phobias, and Panic," engage in "creative neglect," which entails not being available when a friend wishes to hang out or talk.Plan outings with friends who make you happy and want to hang out with. Cloud suggests that one way to appreciate the value of spending time with positive people and doing good things is to volunteer for charities and other non-profit organizations.Even if you are not particularly busy, Levine encourages you to use the excuse if you are comfortable doing so.

Step 4: Be around positive people.Even though it can be difficult to lose a friend, you will have more time to spend with those who improve your life.Cloud suggests using pictures of the people who are worth your time or imagining how their presence will improve your life as a constant reminder of the people who are worth your time.

This will remind you how important it is to have friends who are kind to you and that you shouldn't spend time or energy on people who make you feel bad.

Conclusion

Although verbal abuse does not result in bodily harm, its psychological effects can last a lifetime.Perhaps because of this, it hurts the most when it comes from a family member.Many people believe that yelling and name-calling are the only forms of verbal abuse;However, it frequently does so in much more subtly disguised ways.The first step in responding to verbal abuse is to recognize it.

www.ingramcontent.com/pod-product-compliance
Lightning Source LLC
Chambersburg PA
CBHW060928130726

48001CB00006B/2473